Homemade Ice Cream Recipe Book

60 Easy & Delicious Recipes for Traditional Ice Cream & Frozen Yogurt, Keto & Vegan Frozen Desserts, Granitas & Gelatos, Sorbets & Sherbets, & Ice Cream for Adults

Helen Pearson

© August 2020

© COPYRIGHT 2020 BY HELEN PEARSON

ALL RIGHTS RESERVED

In accordance with the U.S. Copyright Act of 1976, the reproduction, scanning, photocopying, recording, storing in retrieval systems, copying, transmitting, or circulating in any form by any means— electronic, mechanical, or otherwise— any part of this publication without a written permission from the publisher, constitutes piracy or theft of the author's intellectual property rights.

Exceptions only include cases of brief quotations embodied in critical reviews and/or other certain non-commercial uses permitted by copyright law. Alternatively, when using any material from this book other than reviewing simply, obtain prior permission by contacting the author, **Helen Pearson**.

ISBN: 9798671239577

Thank you for supporting the rights of the author and publisher.

NOTARIAL NOTES

The contents presented herein constitute the rights of the First Amendment. All information states to be truthful, accurate, reliable, and consistent. Any liability, by way of inattention or otherwise, to any use or abuse of any policies, processes, or directions contained within, is the sole discretion and responsibility of the recipient reader.

The presentation of the entire information is without a contract or any form of guarantees or assurances. Both author and publisher shall be, in no case, held liable for any fraud or fraudulent misrepresentations, monetary losses, damages, and liabilities—indirect or consequential—arising from event/s beyond reasonable control or relatively set out in this book.

Therefore, any information hereupon solely offers for educational purposes only, and as such, universal. It does not intend to be a diagnosis, prescription, or treatment for any diseases.

The Food and Drug Administration has not evaluated the statements in the book. If advice is necessary, consult a qualified professional for further questions concerning specific or critical matters on the subject.

The trademarks used herein are without any consent. Thus, the publication of the trademark is without any permission or backing by the trademark owner/s.

All trademarks/brands mentioned are for clarification purposes only and owned by the owners themselves not affiliated with the author or publisher.

Table of Contents

Introduction 7
Classic Ice Creams 13
    Vanilla Ice Cream 13
    Peach Ice Cream 16
    Cookies and Cream Ice Cream 20
    Coconut Ice Cream 23
    Chocolate Ice Cream 26
    Strawberry Ice Cream 29
    Coffee Ice Cream 32
    Rhubarb and Strawberry Ice Cream 35
    Fresh Spearmint Ice Cream 38
    Orange Ice Cream 41
    Pumpkin Ice Cream 44
    Avocado Ice Cream 47
    Blueberry No-Churn Ice Cream 50
    Watermelon Ice Cream 53
    Green Tea Matcha Ice Cream 55
Frozen Yogurts 58
    Creamy Vanilla Frozen Yogurt 58
    Blueberry Basil Frozen Yogurt 61
    Mango Lassi Swirl Frozen Yogurt 64
    Strawberry Rhubarb Frozen Yogurt 67
    Green Tea Honey Frozen Yogurt 70

Gelatos 72
    Strawberry Gelato 72
    Classic Gelato 75
    Chocolate Gelato 78
    Homemade Pistachio Gelato 81
    Banana Gelato 84
Granitas 87
    Strawberry Mint Granita 87
    Coffee Granita 90
    Melon Granita 93
    Zesty Lemon Granita 96
    Grapefruit Sparkling Granita 99
Sorbets & Sherbets 102
    Strawberry Sorbet 102
    Peach Sorbet 104
    Pineapple Thai Basil Ginger Sorbet 106
    Coconut Pineapple Sorbet 108
    Mango Sorbet 111
    Orange Sherbet 114
    Amaretto Chocolate Sherbet 118
    Cranberry Sherbet 120
    Watermelon Sherbet 123
    Wild Raspberry Sherbet 126
Keto Low Carb Ice Creams 129
    Low Carb Vanilla Ice Cream 129

- Low Carb Mocha Ice Cream 132
- Brown Butter Pecan Ice Cream 135
- Butterscotch Sea Salt Ice Cream...138
- Low Carb Chocolate Ice Cream 141

Vegan Ice Creams 144
- Watermelon Mint Ice Cream 144
- Vegan Mango Ice Cream... 147
- Vegan Chocolate Ice Cream 149
- Fudgy Marble Fudge Gelato 152
- Chocolate Chunk Beet Ice Cream 155

For Adults 158
- Rum Cherry Ice Cream 158
- Mojito Ice Cream 162
- Moscato Ice Cream 166
- Stout Ice Cream with Bittersweet Hot Fudge.................... 169
- Piña Colada Sorbet 173
- Coffee Rum Ice Cream 175
- Prosecco Ice Cream..178
- Margarita Pops..180
- Mudslide Ice Cream... 183
- Coffee Vodka Ice Cream 186

Conversion Tables 189

Introduction

What is the best summer dessert for kids and adults? Of course, it's ice cream. Fruit, chocolate, vanilla, gelato, sorbet... There are so many flavors and variations. But have you ever thought of making your own homemade ice cream? Do you still wonder if it is worth the trouble? It is!

So what are the advantages of homemade ice cream versus store-bought? First, you know for sure what ingredients it consists of. You will include only natural ingredients in your ice cream and can make it a much healthier option. If you or your kids have allergies, you will be able to modify the recipe and still enjoy your favorite dessert.

You can also create your own flavors. Feel like cherry or avocado ice cream? No need to look for it in a store, just make your own. Most ice cream recipes do not contain many ingredients, so it will be easy to get everything you need.

You can control the sugar intake. Store-bought ice creams usually contain a lot of sugar. By making your own homemade ice cream you can even replace sugar with sweetener, maple syrup, or honey to make it a healthier option.

You can cook diet-friendly ice cream. It is hard to find real low carb, vegan, or protein ice cream in a store, but you can prepare one. By making your own ice cream, you can make it low carb, high protein, or even vegan, just find the best recipe.

What tools and appliances will you need?

- Blender

- Mixer

- Ice cream maker (optional)

- Spatula and whisk

- Airtight containers

There are a few useful tips you can follow to make your homemade ice cream even better.

1. Chill the ice cream mixture before freezing. Just bring it to room temperature and then refrigerate it for 1-2 hours before freezing or processing it in an ice cream-making machine.

2. When preparing custard, pour only 3-4 tablespoons of hot cream or milk into the egg yolks. After that, add the yolks to the hot cream and stir well. Thus, you will not cook scrambled eggs accidentally.

3. If you want to add flavor to ice cream (vanilla, almond extracts), add them to the chilled ice cream mixture before freezing.

4. The best containers for ice cream would be shallow and flat, this will help the ice cream to keep an even consistency.

5. Ice cream will only be good if you use high-quality ingredients. Try to get organic milk and eggs; make sure all the ingredients are fresh.

6. Even if you watch your calorie intake, you will have to use only high-fat ingredients for homemade ice cream as it depends on a high-fat content to get a creamy texture.

7. If you are using an ice cream maker machine for your homemade ice cream, freeze the bowl first. It would be better if you freeze it for 24 hours prior to preparing.

8. Add-ins should be chopped finely. If you add nuts, chocolate chips, or candies to the ice cream, make sure you chop them well before stirring them in.

9. To have a creamier texture of homemade ice cream, add alcohol to it (few tablespoons). Other ingredients like sugar, corn syrup, honey, gelatine, and other commercial stabilizers can also keep a softer consistency of ice cream.

10. To get a finer texture of ice cream, grind coarse sweetener before using.

Storage rules for storing homemade ice cream:

1. Start with checking the temperature of your freezer. It should be zero degrees F or below; this is the best temperature for storing ice cream.

2. Get shallow, flat containers. While ice cream in America is usually sold in tall containers, real Italian ice cream is only stored in shallow flat containers to maintain the consistency.

3. Cover the ice cream with plastic wrap. This will prevent ice crystals from forming. You can also use airtight containers to keep the ice cream covered.

4. Store ready ice cream in the back of the freezer, the temperature there is the coldest. Do not store it in the freezer door.

5. Do not change temperatures too often. Defrost it a little bit before serving and then return it to the freezer. If you melt the ice cream completely, you will need to repeat the churning process again.

Place it in a freezer for 1 hour, then stir well and return it to the freezer for 1-2 hours. Repeat the process 2-3 more times.

6. One of the main rules – store homemade ice cream for no longer than 2 months. Commercial ice creams can be stored for a longer time as they usually contain stabilizers and preservatives.

Classic Ice Creams

Vanilla Ice Cream

Preparation Time: 3-4 hours

Cooking Time: 20 minutes

Servings: 4

Ingredients:

- 3 cups whole milk

- 2 cups heavy cream
- 1/2 cup of sugar
- 5 large egg yolks
- 1/4 teaspoon kosher salt
- 1 vanilla bean

Instructions:

1. Place a skillet over medium heat.
2. Add whole milk, heavy cream, sugar, salt, and vanilla bean to the pan. Cook until hot while stirring often. Scoop out 1 cup of milk and set aside.
3. Add egg yolks to the cup of milk. Pour this into the pan and stir. Cook for 10 minutes until the mixture thickens. Remove from heat and strain the mixture. Discard solids and chill the remaining liquid for 24 hours.

4. Transfer the ice cream mixture to a container and freeze for 40 minutes. After 40 minutes, remove it from the freezer and stir very well with a fork or a spatula.

5. Freeze for another 40 minutes. Repeat the process 3-4 more times or until the ice cream is frozen.

6. Serve and enjoy!

Nutritional information (per serving): 436 calories; 34 g fat; 24 g total carbs; 10 g protein

Peach Ice Cream

Preparation Time: 3-4 hours

Cooking Time: 30 minutes

Servings: 4

Ingredients:

- 1 lb. peaches peeled, pitted, and sliced
- 1 cup heavy cream

- 1 cup whole milk

- 8 large egg yolks

- 3/4 cup of sugar

- 1 tablespoon fresh lemon juice

- 2 teaspoons vanilla extract

- 1/2 teaspoon kosher salt

Instructions:

1. Place a pan over medium-high heat. Heat cream and milk in the pan for about 3 minutes until you can see tiny bubbles.

2. In a large bowl whisk together egg yolks, sugar, and salt until thick and pale in color for 2 minutes.

3. Remove the milk mixture from heat and gradually add it into the egg mixture while constantly. Pour the mixture back into the pan and place over

medium heat. Cook and stir constantly for 7 minutes until the mixture is thick.

4. Sieve the mixture and discard solids. Pour the mixture in a bowl placed in an ice bath.

5. Place a medium saucepan over medium heat. Add peaches and water and bring it to a boil, reduce heat to medium and let it simmer for 12 minutes until softened. Remove and set aside for 5 minutes.

6. Pour the mixture into a blender and blend until formed into a smooth puree. Pour the puree, lemon juice, and vanilla into the cooled custard.

7. Transfer the ice cream mixture to a container and freeze for 40 minutes. After 40 minutes, remove it from the freezer and stir very well with a fork or a spatula.

8. Freeze for another 40 minutes. Repeat the process 3-4 more times or until the ice cream is frozen.

9. Serve and enjoy!

Nutritional information (per serving): 411 calories; 22 g fat; 47 g total carbs; 8 g protein

Cookies and Cream Ice Cream

Preparation Time: 3-4 hours

Cooking Time: 20 minutes

Servings: 4

Ingredients:

- 1.5 cups of skim milk
- 1.5 cups heavy cream

- 2/3 cup of sugar, divided
- 1.75 cups chocolate sandwich cookie pieces, plus more for sprinkling
- 4 large egg yolks
- 1/4 teaspoon coarse salt

Instructions:

1. Place a skillet over medium heat. Add milk, cream, sugar, and salt and bring the mixture to a simmer. Meanwhile, make an ice bath and set aside.
2. In another bowl, whisk together egg yolks and the remaining sugar.
3. Gradually add in half of the milk mixture and whisk. Add the mixture back into the skillet. Cook for 7 minutes, whisk constantly until the mixture thickens. Remove from heat and sieve into the prepared ice-water bath.

4. Transfer the ice cream mixture to a container and freeze for 40 minutes. After 40 minutes, remove it from the freezer, add cookies and stir very well with a fork or a spatula.

5. Freeze for another 40 minutes. Repeat the process 3-4 more times or until the ice cream is frozen.

6. Serve and enjoy!

Nutritional information (per serving): 417 calories; 25 g fat; 43 g total carbs; 8 g protein

Coconut Ice Cream

Preparation Time: 3-4 hours

Cooking Time: 25 minutes

Servings: 4

Ingredients:

- 2 cups skim milk
- 2 cups heavy cream

- 1 cup unsweetened coconut flakes, toasted
- 1 cup of sugar
- 6 large egg yolks
- 1/4 cup shredded sweetened coconut
- 1/4 teaspoon coarse salt

Instructions:

1. Place a skillet over medium heat. Add milk, cream, coconut, and salt to the skillet. Bring the mixture to a simmer, remove from heat, and set aside for 2 hours. Meanwhile, prepare an ice-water bath.
2. Return the mixture to medium heat, add in 1/2 cup of sugar and bring the mixture to a boil.
3. In a medium bowl combine the egg yolks and the remaining 1/2 cup of sugar.
4. Gradually add half of the milk mixture, whisk and pour the mixture back into the pan. Cook until

thick for 6 minutes. Remove from heat, sieve, and place the mixture in an ice-cold bath.

5. Transfer the ice cream mixture to a container and freeze for 40 minutes. After 40 minutes, remove it from the freezer and stir very well with a fork or a spatula.

6. Freeze for another 40 minutes. Repeat the process 3-4 more times or until the ice cream is frozen.

7. Serve ice cream sprinkled with sweetened coconut.

Nutritional information (per serving): 528 calories; 35 g fat; 45 g total carbs; 10 g protein

Chocolate Ice Cream

Preparation Time: 3-4 hours

Cooking Time: 15 minutes

Servings: 4

Ingredients:

- 2.5 cups heavy cream
- 2 cups whole milk

- 3/4 cup of sugar

- 4 oz. melted bittersweet chocolate

- 3 oz. melted milk chocolate

- 8 egg yolks

- 1/4 teaspoon salt

Instructions

1. Place a skillet over medium heat. Add cream, milk, and heat until hot for about 2 minutes. Set aside for 1/2 an hour. Prepare an ice bath.

2. Place sugar, yolks, and salt in a mixer and whisk on high speed for about 3 minutes.

3. Ladle 1 cup cream of the mixture into the yolk mixture and reduce mixing speed to medium. Add another cup of the cream mixture and whisk until combined, then transfer to a saucepan.

4. Place the saucepan over medium-high heat and cook for 7 minutes until the mixture is thick.

5. Add bittersweet and milk chocolate to the saucepan. Remove from heat, sieve it, and place mixture in the ice-cold bath. Let it cool.

6. Transfer the ice cream mixture to a container and freeze for 40 minutes. After 40 minutes, remove it from the freezer and stir very well with a fork or a spatula.

7. Freeze for another 40 minutes. Repeat the process 3-4 more times or until the ice cream is frozen.

8. Serve and enjoy!

Nutritional information (per serving): 616 calories; 42 g fat; 49 g total carbs; 12 g protein

Strawberry Ice Cream

Preparation Time: 3-4 hours

Cooking Time: 18 minutes

Servings: 4

Ingredients

- 6 large egg yolks
- 3/4 cup + 1/4 cup of sugar

- 1.5 cups of skim milk
- 3 cups sliced strawberries
- 1.5 cups heavy cream
- 1/7 teaspoon coarse salt

Instructions

1. In a skillet whisk together egg yolks, sugar, and salt. Gradually whisk in milk.
2. Place the skillet over medium-high heat, stir the mixture until it thickens for 12 minutes. Remove from heat, sieve the custard into a bowl.
3. Add cream to the bowl, set aside, and stir occasionally until chilled.
4. In a separate bowl, mash the strawberries and 1/4 cup of sugar. Set aside for 10 minutes.
5. Combine the strawberry mixture with the ice cream. Transfer the ice cream mixture to a

container and freeze for 40 minutes. After 40 minutes, remove it from the freezer and stir very well with a fork or a spatula.

6. Freeze for another 40 minutes. Repeat the process 3-4 more times or until the ice cream is frozen.

7. Serve and enjoy!

Nutritional information (per serving): 400 calories; 24 g fat; 40 g total carbs; 9 g protein

Coffee Ice Cream

Preparation Time: 3-4 hours

Cooking Time: 20 minutes

Servings: 4

Ingredients

- 6 large egg yolks
- 3/4 cup of sugar

- 1.5 cups skim milk
- 1/4 cup crushed espresso beans
- 1.5 cups heavy cream
- 1/6 teaspoon coarse salt

Instructions

1. In a skillet whisk in egg yolks, sugar, and salt.
2. Slowly add in the milk. Place the skillet over medium-high heat. Cook for 12 minutes until the custard thickens.
3. Add in 1/4 cup crushed espresso beans. Cover and set aside for 1/2 hour.
4. Sieve the mixture into a bowl and place it over an ice bath until chilled. Do not forget to stir often.
5. Transfer the ice cream mixture to a container and freeze for 40 minutes. After 40 minutes, remove it

from the freezer and stir very well with a fork or a spatula.

6. Freeze for another 40 minutes. Repeat the process 3-4 more times or until the ice cream is frozen.

7. Serve and enjoy!

Nutritional information (per serving): 342 calories; 24 g fat; 25 g total carbs; 8 g protein

Rhubarb and Strawberry Ice Cream

Preparation Time: 3-4 hours

Cooking Time: 30 minutes

Servings: 4

Ingredients

- 3.5 trimmed rhubarb, cut into cubes
- 3/4 cup + 2 tablespoons sugar

- 8 oz. ripe strawberries
- 1 cup heavy cream
- 1/2 cup milk
- 2 tablespoons water
- 2 tablespoons kirsch

Instructions

1. Place a skillet over medium heat. Add rhubarb, 1/2 cup of sugar, and water. Bring to a boil, reduce heat to low, and continue to stir for 12 minutes until the rhubarb starts to fall apart. Transfer to a bowl and set aside.
2. Add strawberries to a blender and blend until a smooth puree is formed. Sieve it and place it into a bowl.
3. Add the milk and cream to a small saucepan. Place over medium heat, do not let it boil. Remove from heat.

4. Add 6 tablespoons sugar to the milk, whisk until it's all dissolved. Set aside to cool.

5. In a large bowl combine rhubarb, strawberry puree, cream mixture, and kirsch.

6. Transfer the ice cream mixture to a container and freeze for 40 minutes. After 40 minutes, remove it from the freezer and stir very well with a fork or a spatula.

7. Freeze for another 40 minutes. Repeat the process 3-4 more times or until the ice cream is frozen.

8. Serve and enjoy!

Nutritional information (per serving): 345 calories; 12 g fat; 61 g total carbs; 2 g protein

Fresh Spearmint Ice Cream

Preparation Time: 3-4 hours

Cooking Time: 25 minutes

Servings: 4

Ingredients

- 1 cup packed fresh spearmint
- 1 cup of water

- 1 cup whole milk

- 2 cups heavy cream

- 3/4 cup of sugar

- 2 eggs

Instructions

1. Place a saucepan over medium heat. Add water and bring it to a boil.

2. Add mint to the pan and cook it until it turns bright green. Remove from heat, cool, drain and squeeze out excess liquid. Prepare an ice-water bath and set aside.

3. Add the mint and milk to a blender. Puree until smooth and transfer the mixture to the saucepan placed over medium heat.

4. Add cream to the saucepan and bring the mixture to a simmer.

5. In a separate bowl, whisk eggs and sugar. Gradually add 1/3 of the cream-mint mixture, then add back to the saucepan. Cook while stirring constantly until the mixture thickens for about 8-10 minutes. Remove from heat, sieve it in a clean bowl and set it in the prepared ice bath.

6. Transfer the ice cream mixture to a container and freeze for 40 minutes. After 40 minutes, remove it from the freezer and stir very well with a fork or a spatula.

7. Freeze for another 40 minutes. Repeat the process 3-4 more times or until the ice cream is frozen.

8. Serve and enjoy!

Nutritional information (per serving): 360 calories; 26 g fat; 25 g total carbs; 7 g protein

Orange Ice Cream

Preparation Time: 3-4 hours

Cooking Time: 20 minutes

Servings: 4

Ingredients

- 8 egg yolks
- 1 cup of sugar

- 2 cups skim milk
- 2 cups heavy cream
- 6 strips orange zest
- 1/4 teaspoon coarse salt

Instructions

1. In a skillet, whisk egg yolks, sugar, and salt. Slowly add in milk.
2. Place skillet over medium heat, stir the mixture constantly for about 10 minutes until the custard thickens.
3. Add in the orange zest. Remove from heat and set aside for about 1/2 an hour.
4. Sieve the mixture, place it in a bowl, and stir in the cream. Set aside to cool and keep stirring frequently.

5. Transfer the ice cream mixture to a container and freeze for 40 minutes. After 40 minutes, remove it from the freezer and stir very well with a fork or a spatula.

6. Freeze for another 40 minutes. Repeat the process 3-4 more times or until the ice cream is frozen.

7. Serve and enjoy!

Nutritional information (per serving): 456 calories; 31 g fat; 34 g total carbs; 11 g protein

Pumpkin Ice Cream

Preparation Time: 3-4 hours

Cooking Time: 20 minutes

Servings: 4

Ingredients

- 1 can pumpkin puree (15-oz.)
- 2 cups whole milk

- 2 cups heavy cream

- 1 cup packed brown sugar

- 6 egg yolks

- 1 teaspoon pure vanilla extract

- 1 teaspoon cinnamon

- 1/2 teaspoon ginger

- 1/2 teaspoon nutmeg

- 1/4 teaspoon kosher salt

Instructions

1. Place a skillet over medium heat. In the skillet whisk in pumpkin puree, milk, and cream. Bring it to a boil and remove from heat.

2. In a large bowl combine brown sugar and egg yolks for 4 minutes until pale and thick ribbons form.

3. Slowly whisk in 1/2 cup of the hot pumpkin mixture. Pour back into the skillet with the rest of the pumpkin mixture. Reduce heat to low, stir frequently for about 5 minutes until mixture thickens.

4. Add in vanilla and spices. Remove from heat and sieve the custard into a bowl. Place the bowl in an ice bath, let it chill for 3 hours, covered.

5. Transfer the ice cream mixture to a container and freeze for 40 minutes. After 40 minutes, remove it from the freezer and stir very well with a fork or a spatula.

6. Freeze for another 40 minutes. Repeat the process 3-4 more times or until the ice cream is frozen.

7. Serve and enjoy!

Nutritional information (per serving): 606 calories; 33 g fat; 70 g total carbs; 10 g protein

Avocado Ice Cream

Preparation Time: 3-4 hours

Cooking Time: 5 minutes

Servings: 4

Ingredients

- 2 avocados, peeled and pitted
- 1/2 cup lime juice

- zest of 1 lime
- 1/2 cup maple syrup
- 1 can coconut cream
- 1 teaspoon vanilla extract
- 1 tablespoon coconut oil
- 1/4 teaspoon kosher salt
- 1/4 lime, thinly sliced into quarters, for garnish

Instructions

1. In a blender combine avocados, lime juice, lime zest, maple syrup, coconut cream, vanilla extract, coconut oil, and salt. Blend until smooth. Pour the mixture in a loaf pan, garnish with lime slices.

2. Transfer the ice cream mixture to a container and freeze for 40 minutes. After 40 minutes, remove it from the freezer and stir very well with a fork or a spatula.

3. Freeze for another 40 minutes. Repeat the process 3-4 more times or until the ice cream is frozen.

4. Serve and enjoy!

Nutritional information (per serving): 397 calories; 28 g fat; 40 g total carbs; 3 g protein

Blueberry No-Churn Ice Cream

Preparation Time: 3-4 hours

Cooking Time: 20 minutes

Servings: 4

Ingredients

- 4 cups blueberries, plus more for serving
- 1/4 cup granulated sugar

- 3 cups heavy cream
- 1 can sweetened condensed milk (14-oz.)
- 3 tablespoons lemon juice
- zest of 1 lemon

Instructions

1. Add 4 cups blueberries to a blender and blend until a smooth puree is formed.
2. Add the puree to a saucepan placed over medium heat.
3. Add sugar, lemon juice, and lemon zest to the saucepan. Bring to a boil, then reduce heat and let it simmer for about 15 minutes.
4. In a separate bowl, add the cream. Beat the cream using your hand mixer until stiff peaks form.
5. Fold in the sweetened condensed milk, then fold in the pureed mixture.

6. Transfer the ice cream mixture to a container. Freeze it for 40 minutes. After 40 minutes, remove it from the freezer and stir very well with a fork or a spatula.

7. Freeze for another 40 minutes. Repeat the process 2-4 more times or until the ice cream is frozen.

8. Once done, serve with fresh blueberries.

Nutritional information (per serving): 884 calories; 43 g fat; 121 g total carbs; 11 g protein

Watermelon Ice Cream

Preparation Time: 3-4 hours

Cooking Time: 0 minutes

Servings: 4

Ingredients

- 2 cups cubed watermelon
- 2 cups whole milk

- 2 tablespoons sugar

- 1/4 teaspoon pure vanilla extract

Instructions

1. Add the cubed watermelon, milk, sugar, vanilla extract to a blender, and blend.

2. Pour the mixture into a loaf pan.

3. Transfer the ice cream mixture to a container. Freeze it for 40 minutes. After 40 minutes, remove it from the freezer and stir very well with a fork or a spatula or blend with a blender again.

4. Freeze for another 40 minutes. Repeat the process 2-4 more times or until the ice cream is frozen.

5. Serve and enjoy!

Nutritional information (per serving): 114 calories; 4 g fat; 16 g total carbs; 4 g protein

Green Tea Matcha Ice Cream

Preparation Time: 3-4 hours

Cooking Time: 10 minutes

Servings: 4

Ingredients

- 3/4 cup whole milk
- 3/4 cup heavy cream, whipped

- 2 egg yolks

- 1 tablespoon matcha green tea powder

- 3 tablespoons hot water

- 5 tablespoons granulated white sugar

Instructions

1. Combine hot water and matcha tea powder in a medium bowl, set aside.

2. In a skillet, whisk the egg yolks. Slowly add sugar and mix well.

3. Slowly add milk to the pan and whisk well.

4. Place pan over medium-low heat, stir the mixture constantly until it thickens.

5. Pour the mixture into a bowl, place the bowl in an ice bath, stir to cool.

6. Add matcha powder and the water mixture to the egg mixture. Stir until cool in the ice bath.

7. In a separate bowl, whip the heavy cream until slightly thick and airy using a hand mixer. Fold this into the matcha mixture.

8. Transfer the ice cream mixture to a container and freeze for 40 minutes. After 40 minutes, remove it from the freezer and stir very well with a fork or a spatula.

9. Freeze for another 40 minutes. Repeat the process 3-4 more times or until the ice cream is frozen.

10. Serve and enjoy!

Nutritional information (per serving): 187 calories; 14 g fat; 13 g total carbs; 4 g protein

Frozen Yogurts

Creamy Vanilla Frozen Yogurt

Preparation Time: 3-4 hours

Cooking Time: 5 minutes

Servings: 4

Ingredients

- 3 cups plain 2 percent reduced-fat Greek-style yogurt
- 2 cups half-and-half
- 2/3 cups sugar
- 1/3 cups light corn syrup
- 1.5 teaspoon vanilla extract
- 1/4 teaspoons Kosher salt

Instructions

1. In a large bowl whisk yogurt, half-and-half, sugar, syrup, vanilla extract, and salt. Combine for 5 minutes until sugar dissolves.

2. Transfer the ice cream mixture to a container and freeze overnight or for at least 6 hours.

3. Serve and enjoy!

Nutritional information (per serving): 334 calories; 4 g fat; 62 g total carbs; 13 g protein

Blueberry Basil Frozen Yogurt

Preparation Time: 3-4 hours

Cooking Time: 0 minutes

Servings: 4

Ingredients

- 3/4 cup of fresh basil leaves, whole
- 2 cups half-and-half

- 3 cups plain 2 percent Greek-style yogurt
- 2/3 cup of sugar
- 1/3 cup light corn syrup
- 1.5 teaspoons pure vanilla extract
- 1.5 cups blueberries
- 1/2 cup blueberry preserves
- 3 tablespoons chopped fresh basil
- 1 tablespoon lemon zest
- 1/4 teaspoon kosher salt

Instructions

1. In a bowl combine basil leaves with half-and-half. Set in the fridge to chill for 24 hours. Sieve to discard the basil.
2. In another separate bowl combine yogurt, corn syrup, sugar, vanilla, salt, and half-and-half.

Whisk until sugar dissolves, set aside for 5 minutes. Place in the freezer and chill for 2 hours.

3. In a separate bowl, mash blueberries, blueberry preserves, chopped basil, and lemon zest. Pour this to the yogurt mixture.

4. Transfer the ice cream mixture to a container and freeze overnight or for at least 6 hours.

5. Serve and enjoy!

Nutritional information (per serving): 435 calories; 2.5 g fat; 92 g total carbs; 14 g protein

Mango Lassi Swirl Frozen Yogurt

Preparation Time: 3-4 hours

Cooking Time: 0 minutes

Servings: 4

Ingredients

- 3 cups plain 2 percent reduced-fat Greek-style yogurt

- 2 cups half-and-half
- 2/3 cup of sugar
- 1/3 cup light corn syrup
- 3/4 cup mango jam
- 3/4 cup chopped fresh mango
- 1.5 teaspoon vanilla extract
- 1/4 teaspoon kosher salt
- 1 tablespoon lime zest

Instructions

1. In a large bowl, combine yogurt, half-and-half, sugar, corn syrup, vanilla, and salt. Set it aside for 5 minutes. Whisk until sugar dissolves, place in the refrigerator to chill for 2 hours.

2. Add the mango jam and chopped mango to a food processor and pulse until smooth.

3. Add the mango mixture and lime zest to the yogurt.

4. Transfer the ice cream mixture to a container and freeze overnight or for at least 6 hours.

5. Serve and enjoy!

Nutritional information (per serving): 360 calories; 2.3 g fat; 73 g total carbs; 14 g protein

Strawberry Rhubarb Frozen Yogurt

Preparation Time: 3-4 hours

Cooking Time: 10 minutes

Servings: 4

Ingredients

- 3 cups plain 2 percent reduced-fat Greek-style yogurt

- 2 cups half-and-half
- 1 cup of sugar, divided
- 1/3 cup light corn syrup
- 2 cups fresh strawberries
- 1 cup rhubarb, chopped
- 1.5 teaspoon vanilla extract
- 1/4 teaspoon kosher salt

Instructions

1. In a large bowl whisk yogurt, half-and-half, 2/3 cups sugar, corn syrup, vanilla, and salt. Set aside for 5 minutes. Whisk until sugar dissolves, chill in the refrigerator for 2 hours.

2. Place a skillet over medium heat. Add fresh strawberries and rhubarb to the pan and 1/3 cup of sugar and cook for 8 minutes until the strawberries are tender. Remove from heat.

3. Add the strawberry mixture to the yogurt mixture.

4. Transfer the ice cream mixture to a container and freeze overnight or for at least 6 hours.

5. Serve and enjoy!

Nutritional information (per serving): 458 calories; 4.8 g fat; 94 g total carbs; 13 g protein

Green Tea Honey Frozen Yogurt

Preparation Time: 3-4 hours

Cooking Time: 0 minutes

Servings: 4

Ingredients

- 3 cups plain Greek yogurt
- 2 cups half-and-half

- 2/3 cup of sugar
- 1/3 cup honey
- 3 tablespoons matcha green tea powder
- 1.5 teaspoons vanilla extract
- 1/4 teaspoon kosher salt

Instructions

1. In a large bowl combine yogurt, half-and-half, sugar, honey, matcha, vanilla, and salt. Set aside for 5 minutes. Whisk until sugar dissolves, then refrigerate for 2 hours.
2. Transfer the ice cream mixture to a container and freeze overnight or for at least 6 hours.
3. Serve and enjoy!

Nutritional information (per serving): 340 calories; 4.5 g fat; 53 g total carbs; 13 g protein

Gelatos

Strawberry Gelato

Preparation Time: 3-4 hours

Cooking Time: 0 minutes

Servings: 4

Ingredients

- 1 lb. fresh strawberries, cleaned, stems and leaves removed
- 1 cup granulated sugar
- 3/4 cup of water
- 1/2 cup heavy whipping cream
- 2 tablespoons freshly squeezed lemon juice

Instructions

1. Add strawberries, lemon juice, and sugar to a blender. Process until liquefied.
2. Add water to the blender and process until smooth.
3. In a separate bowl, add the cream. Whip it with a whisk until it thickens slightly.
4. Add the strawberry mixture to the whipped cream.

5. Transfer the ice cream mixture to a container and freeze for 40 minutes. After 40 minutes, remove it from the freezer and stir very well with a fork or a spatula.

6. Freeze for another 40 minutes. Repeat the process 3-4 more times or until the ice cream is frozen.

7. Serve and enjoy!

Nutritional information (per serving): 167 calories; 5 g fat; 30 g total carbs; 6 g protein

Classic Gelato

Preparation Time: 3-4 hours

Cooking Time: 15 minutes

Servings: 4

Ingredients

- 1 cup heavy cream
- 2 cups of milk

- 1/2 cup of sugar

- 4 egg yolks

Instructions

1. Add milk and cream to a pan and mix. Heat until foam is formed, then remove from heat.

2. Add egg yolks and sugar to a bowl and beat until frothy.

3. Add warm milk to the egg yolks and whisk. Then return the mixture to the pan, heat over medium heat, stirring until the mixture thickens a little. Once thickened, remove from heat. Sieve into a container.

4. Transfer the ice cream mixture to a container and freeze for 40 minutes. After 40 minutes, remove it from the freezer and stir very well with a fork or a spatula.

5. Freeze for another 40 minutes. Repeat the process 3-4 more times or until the ice cream is frozen.

6. Serve and enjoy!

Nutritional information (per serving): 415 calories; 29 g fat; 33 g total carbs; 8 g protein

Chocolate Gelato

Preparation Time: 3-4 hours

Cooking Time: 10 minutes

Servings: 4

Ingredients

- 4 oz. bittersweet chocolate, finely chopped
- 3 cups organic whole milk

- 2 egg yolks
- 3/4 cup granulated organic cane sugar
- 1/2 cup unsweetened cocoa powder
- 1.5 tablespoons cornstarch powder
- 1/2 teaspoon vanilla extract
- 1/4 teaspoon sea salt

Instructions

1. Prepare the ice-water bath. Add chocolate to a microwave-safe bowl. Melt in a microwave and set aside.
2. Place a pan over medium heat. Add milk and bring it to a simmer.
3. In a separate bowl, combine yolks, sugar, and salt until it turns pale in color.
4. Add in cocoa powder and cornstarch until a paste is formed.

5. Gradually add hot milk to the cocoa mixture, mix until smooth. Return the mixture to pan and heat over medium heat. Frequently stir the mixture for 5 minutes until it thickens.

6. Strain the mixture and add melted chocolate. Stir and add vanilla and place it into the ice bath. Let it chill and keep stirring.

7. Transfer the ice cream mixture to a container and freeze for 40 minutes. After 40 minutes, remove it from the freezer and stir very well with a fork or a spatula.

8. Freeze for another 40 minutes. Repeat the process 3-4 more times or until the ice cream is frozen.

9. Serve and enjoy!

Nutritional information (per serving): 314 calories; 12 g fat; 49 g total carbs; 7 g protein

Homemade Pistachio Gelato

Preparation Time: 3-4 hours

Cooking Time: 10 minutes

Servings: 4

Ingredients

- 2 cups 2% milk
- 1 cup heavy whipping cream

- 4 egg yolks

- 1/2 cup of sugar

- 1/3 cup pistachio nut paste

- 1/3 cup shelled and roasted pistachios

Instructions

1. Place a skillet over medium heat. Add milk and whipping cream and let it simmer.

2. In a medium bowl combine egg yolks and sugar, whisk until the mixture is smooth.

3. Remove the skillet from heat, scoop out half of the milk mixture and gradually whisk it in the egg yolk mixture, transfer this mixture to the skillet and add it to the milk mixture. Cook slowly while stirring frequently.

4. Add pistachio nut paste to the skillet. Continue cooking until the mixture thickens, remove the

mixture from the heat and pour it in a bread pan, then let it chill in the freezer for 1/2 an hour.

5. Transfer the ice cream mixture to a container and freeze for 40 minutes. After 40 minutes, remove it from the freezer and stir very well with a fork or a spatula.

6. Freeze for another 40 minutes. Repeat the process 3-4 more times or until the ice cream is frozen.

7. Remove the ice cream from the freezer and set aside at room temperature for 10 minutes.

8. Sprinkle pistachio nuts on the gelato and serve.

Nutritional information (per serving): 475 calories; 33 g fat; 35 g total carbs; 10 g protein

Banana Gelato

Preparation Time: 5-6 hours

Cooking Time: 40 minutes

Servings: 2

Ingredients:

- 1 ripe banana, mashed
- 1/2 can coconut milk

- 1/3 cup of white sugar

- 1 can coconut cream

- 1 teaspoon vanilla extract

Instructions:

1. Add coconut milk and sugar to a saucepan and heat on a low heat until the sugar has dissolved. Bring everything to a low simmer over low heat. Simmer for 30-40 minutes. Remove from heat and let cool completely. Refrigerate.

2. Whip up the coconut cream until fluffy. Add the coconut milk mixture and whip it until thickened. Add vanilla extract.

3. Add the mashed banana and stir well to combine. Refrigerate for 1-2 hours.

4. Transfer the ice cream mixture to a container and freeze for 40 minutes. After 40 minutes, remove it

from the freezer and stir very well with a fork or a spatula.

5. Freeze for another 40 minutes. Repeat the process 3-4 more times or until the ice cream is frozen.

6. Remove the ice cream from the freezer and set aside at room temperature for 10 minutes.

7. Serve and enjoy!

Nutritional Info (per serving): 345 calories; 22 g fat; 24 g total carbs; 8 g protein

Granitas

Strawberry Mint Granita

Preparation Time: 3-4 hours

Cooking Time: 10 minutes

Servings: 4

Ingredients

- 1 cup golden caster sugar

- 1/2 cup of water

- 2 cups strawberries, hulled and halved

- 8 mint leaves, plus extra sprigs to serve

Instructions

1. Place a skillet over low heat. Add sugar and water to the skillet, stir until the sugar dissolves, do not let it boil.

2. Add strawberries to a blender and pulse until it becomes a smooth puree. Pour into the skillet.

3. Add mint leaves and increase the heat to medium heat. Let it simmer for 5 minutes until the mixture thickens. Sieve the mixture and place it in a bowl, allow it to cool for 15 minutes.

4. Transfer the ice cream mixture to a container and freeze for 40 minutes. After 40 minutes, remove it

from the freezer and stir very well with a fork or a spatula.

5. Freeze for another 40 minutes. Repeat the process 3-4 more times or until ice cream is frozen.

6. Serve in tall glasses. Place a sprig of mint on top.

Nutritional information (per serving): 135 calories; 0 g fat; 31 g total carbs; 1 g protein

Coffee Granita

Preparation Time: 3-4 hours

Cooking Time: 0 minutes

Servings: 4

Ingredients

- 2.5 cups freshly brewed, strong black coffee
- 3/8 cup golden caster sugar

- 3 oz. coffee liqueur
- 1 tub mascarpone
- 4 tablespoons dark chocolate, grated

Instructions

1. In a large bowl combine coffee and sugar. Whisk well until the sugar has dissolved.
2. Add coffee liqueur to the bowl, set aside to cool.
3. Transfer ice cream mixture to a container and freeze for 40 minutes. After 40 minutes, remove it from the freezer and stir very well with a fork or a spatula.
4. Freeze for another 40 minutes. Repeat the process 3-4 more times or until the ice cream is frozen.
5. Serve the granita in small serving bowls or glasses, add a dollop of mascarpone and a sprinkle of dark chocolate.

Nutritional information (per serving): 112 calories; 0 g fat; 21 g total carbs; 0.2 g protein

Melon Granita

Preparation Time: 3-4 hours

Cooking Time: 10 minutes

Servings: 4

Ingredients

- 1/2 cup caster sugar
- 1/2 cup of water

- 1 vanilla pod, split
- 2 very ripe Charentais (orange-fleshed) melons
- 1 tablespoon lemon juice

Instructions

1. Add water and sugar to a saucepan. Add one vanilla pod. Place the saucepan over medium-low heat.
2. Heat until the sugar has dissolved, bring to a boil; the process takes about 8 minutes.
3. Remove from heat when a sugar syrup forms, remove the vanilla pod, and set aside to cool.
4. Cut the melons into halves, discard the seeds, then scoop out the flesh and place it on a chopping board.
5. Add the melon to a blender along with the lemon juice and blend for 1 minute, transfer to the cooled sugar syrup.

6. Transfer to a loaf pan and place it into the freezer. Freeze for 60 minutes until crystals form, stir the edges with a fork, and return to the freezer.

7. Repeat the above process every 1 hour about 3-4 times.

8. Serve and enjoy!

Nutritional information (per serving): 69 calories; 0 g fat; 18 g total carbs; 1 g protein

Zesty Lemon Granita

Preparation time: 3-4 hours

Cooking Time: 10 minutes

Servings: 4

Ingredients

- 1 cup of water
- 2/3 cup of sugar

- 2/3 cup lemon juice
- 2 fresh thyme sprigs
- 2 tablespoons lemon zest

Instructions

1. Place a skillet over medium heat. Add water and sugar and bring it to a boil. Stir the sugar with a wooden spoon until it has dissolved. Remove from heat.
2. Add lemon juice and thyme sprigs. Stir well. Transfer to a bowl and let the mixture cool.
3. Transfer the ice cream mixture to a container and freeze for 40 minutes. After 40 minutes, remove it from the freezer and stir very well with a fork or a spatula.
4. Freeze for another 40 minutes. Repeat the process 3-4 more times or until the ice cream is frozen.
5. Serve and garnish with lemon zest. Enjoy!

Nutritional Info (per serving): 140 calories; 0 g fat; 37 g total carbs; 0 g protein

Grapefruit Sparkling Granita

Preparation time: 3-4 hours

Cooking Time: 10 minutes

Servings: 4

Ingredients

- 1 cup grapefruit juice, freshly squeezed
- 1/2 cup of sugar

- 1 cup water

- 1 cup rose Champagne

- A pinch of pink salt

Instructions

1. Place a saucepan over medium heat. Add water and sugar and bring it to a boil. Stir the sugar with a wooden spoon until it has dissolved. Remove from heat.

2. Add grapefruit juice, champagne, and salt. Stir well. Transfer to a bowl and let the mixture cool.

3. Transfer the ice cream mixture to a container and freeze for 40 minutes. After 40 minutes, remove it from the freezer and stir very well with a fork or a spatula.

4. Freeze for another 40 minutes. Repeat the process 3-4 more times or until the ice cream is frozen.

5. Serve and garnish with grapefruit zest. Enjoy!

Nutritional Info (per serving): 134 calories; 0 g fat; 28 g total carbs; 1 g protein

Sorbets & Sherbets

Strawberry Sorbet

Preparation time: 8 hours

Cooking Time: 0 minutes

Servings: 4

Ingredients

- 3 cups strawberries
- 2 tablespoons raw honey
- 1 teaspoon lemon juice
- 1/4 cup of warm water

Instructions

1. Spread strawberries on a parchment-lined baking pan. Freeze for 4 hours.
2. Add the frozen strawberries to a blender, add honey and lemon juice. Pulse until smooth.
3. Add a bit of warm water and blend. Transfer to a container and freeze for 4 hours until firm.
4. Serve and enjoy!

Nutritional Info (per serving): 80 calories; 0.6 g fat; 19.8 g total carbs; 1.1 g protein

Peach Sorbet

Preparation time: 8 hours

Cooking Time: 0 minutes

Servings: 4

Ingredients

- 4 peaches, sliced
- 1 tablespoon raw honey

- 1 teaspoon lemon juice
- 1/2 cup of warm water

Instructions

1. Spread peach slices on a parchment-lined baking sheet. Freeze for 4 hours.
2. Add frozen peach slices to a food processor and pulse until smooth.
3. Add lemon juice, warm water, honey and continue to pulse until smooth.
4. Transfer to an airtight container and freeze for 4 hours until firm.
5. Serve and enjoy!

Nutritional Info (per serving): 80 calories; 0.6 g fat; 19.8 g total carbs; 1.1 g protein

Pineapple Thai Basil Ginger Sorbet

Preparation time: 5-6 hours

Cooking Time: 0 minutes

Servings: 4

Ingredients

- 1 pineapple, peeled, cored, and cut into chunks
- 1 cup of water

- 3/8 cup of white caster sugar
- 1 lime, juiced and zested
- 1 knob ginger, sliced
- A handful of Thai basil leaves

Instructions

1. Add all the ingredients to a blender, pulse until smooth. Transfer the ice cream mixture to a large container and freeze for 4 hours or overnight.
2. Remove the mixture from the freezer, break it into chunks and add it to a blender, process until smooth. Transfer it back to the container and freeze for 1 hour.
3. Serve in bowls, top with extra basil. Enjoy!

Nutritional Info (per serving): 145 calories; 0 g fat; 33 g total carbs; 1 g protein

Coconut Pineapple Sorbet

Preparation time: 4-5 hours

Cooking Time: 10 minutes

Servings: 4

Ingredients:

- 1/2 can coconut milk
- 3/4 cup of white sugar

- 3/4 cup of water

- 2 tablespoons lime juice

- 1/2 can crushed pineapple, drained

Instructions:

1. Mix water and sugar in a saucepan and place it over medium heat. Bring to a boil and stir well until the sugar dissolves. Remove from heat and cool completely.

2. Add the pineapple to a blender and process until smooth. Mix the pineapple puree, syrup, lime juice, and coconut milk together.

3. Transfer the ice cream mixture to a large container and freeze for 4 hours or overnight.

4. Remove the mixture from the freezer, break it into chunks and add it to a blender, process until smooth. Transfer it back to the container and freeze for 1 hour.

5. Serve in bowls. Enjoy!

Nutritional Info (per serving): 156 calories; 4 g fat; 16 g total carbs; 2 g protein

Mango Sorbet

Preparation time: 5-6 hours

Cooking Time: 10 minutes

Servings: 4

Ingredients

- 2 mangos, ripe, peeled, and chopped
- 1/2 cup of sugar

- 1/2 cup of water

- 2 tablespoons lime juice

- 2 tablespoons light corn syrup

- A pinch of salt

Instructions

1. Preheat a pan over medium heat, add sugar, water, and salt, cook until sugar is dissolved.

2. Add mango, lime juice, and sugar mixture to a blender and puree well. Add corn syrup and stir to combine.

3. Transfer the ice cream mixture to a large container and freeze for 4 hours or overnight.

4. Remove the mixture from the freezer, break it into chunks and add it to a blender, process until smooth. Transfer it back to the container and freeze for 1 hour.

5. Serve in bowls. Enjoy!

Nutritional Info (per serving): 216 calories; 8.1 g fat; 35.5 g total carbs; 2 g protein

Orange Sherbet

Preparation time: 5-6 hours

Cooking Time: 0 minutes

Servings: 4

Ingredients

- 1/4 cup of cold water
- 1 teaspoon unflavored gelatin

- 3/4 cup boiling water
- 3/4 cup of sugar
- 2.25 tablespoons orange zest
- 1/2 cup of orange juice
- 1/4 cup lemon juice
- 1 egg yolk, beaten
- 1/2 cup heavy cream
- 3 tablespoons sugar
- 1 pinch salt
- 1 egg white

Instructions

1. Add cold water to a small bowl, sprinkle with gelatin and set aside for 5 minutes.

2. In a separate bowl, combine boiling water, 3/4 cup of sugar, and the soaked gelatin. Stir until the gelatin and sugar dissolve.

3. Stir in the orange zest, orange juice, lemon juice, and egg yolk to the gelatin mixture. Set aside.

4. In another large bowl whip heavy cream, salt, and 3 tablespoons sugar until peaks form.

5. In another medium bowl, whisk the egg white until stiff, fold it into the whipped cream. Gradually add in the juice mixture and mix well to combine.

6. Transfer the ice cream mixture to a large container and freeze for 4 hours or overnight.

7. Remove the mixture from the freezer, break it into chunks and add it to a blender, process until smooth. Transfer it back to the container and freeze for 1 hour.

8. Serve in glasses. Enjoy!

Nutritional Info (per serving): 216 calories; 8.1 g fat; 35.5 g total carbs; 2 g protein

Amaretto Chocolate Sherbet

Preparation time: 5-6 hours

Cooking Time: 0 minutes

Servings: 4

Ingredients

- 1 cup of sugar
- 3/4 cup unsweetened cocoa powder

- 1.5 cups water

- 2 tablespoons amaretto (almond-flavored liqueur)

Instructions

1. In a bowl whisk together sugar, cocoa, water, and amaretto until smooth.

2. Transfer the ice cream mixture to a large container and freeze for 4 hours or overnight.

3. Remove the mixture from the freezer, break it into chunks and add it to a blender, process until smooth. Transfer it back to the container and freeze for 1 hour.

4. Serve and enjoy!

Nutritional Info (per serving): 130 calories; 1.1 g fat; 31.2 g total carbs; 1.6 g protein

Cranberry Sherbet

Preparation time: 5-6 hours

Cooking Time: 5-10 minutes

Servings: 4

Ingredients

- 2 cups fresh cranberries
- 2 cups white sugar

- 2 cups of milk

- 1 cup heavy cream

Instructions

1. Add cranberries to a skillet. Cover with tap water.

2. Place over medium heat and bring to a boil and cook until the cranberries pop. Remove from heat and drain excess water.

3. Return to the saucepan, add in sugar, and cook over low heat. Dissolve the sugar. Transfer to a bowl and chill in a freezer until cold.

4. Add milk and heavy cream. Transfer the ice cream mixture to a large container and freeze for 4 hours or overnight.

5. Remove the mixture from the freezer, break it into chunks and add it to a blender, process until smooth. Transfer it back to the container and freeze for 1 hour.

6. Serve and enjoy!

Nutritional Info (per serving): 337 calories; 12.2 g fat; 56.6 g total carbs; 2.7 g protein

Watermelon Sherbet

Preparation time: 5-6 hours

Cooking Time: 5 minutes

Servings: 4

Ingredients

- 4 cups seedless watermelon, diced
- 1 cup of white sugar

- 1/4 cup of cold water

- 1 envelope (0.25 oz.) unflavored gelatin

- 1 cup heavy cream, chilled

- 3 tablespoons lemon juice

- 1 pinch of salt

Instructions

1. In a large bowl combine watermelon, sugar, lemon juice, and salt. Cover with plastic wrap, place it in the refrigerator for 1/2 an hour.

2. Add the watermelon mixture to a blender and blend until smooth. Set aside in a bowl.

3. Add cold water to a saucepan. Sprinkle with gelatin and set aside for 2 minutes.

4. Place the saucepan over low heat and cook for 2 minutes. Transfer the mixture to the watermelon mixture.

5. Add heavy cream to the same bowl, whisk at medium speed with an electric hand mixer until fluffy.

6. Transfer the ice cream mixture to a large container and freeze for 4 hours or overnight.

7. Remove the mixture from the freezer, break it into chunks and add it to a blender, process until smooth. Transfer it back to the container and freeze for 1 hour.

8. Serve and enjoy!

Nutritional Info (per serving): 226 calories; 11.1 g fat; 32.1 g total carbs; 1.8 g protein

Wild Raspberry Sherbet

Preparation time: 5-6 hours

Cooking Time: 5 minutes

Servings: 4

Ingredients

- 2 cups of wild raspberries
- 1/4 cup of white sugar

- 1.5 cups milk

- 1/4 teaspoon lemon juice

- 1/8 teaspoon ground cinnamon

Instructions

1. Place a skillet over low heat. Add raspberries and sugar, stir with a wooden spoon until sugar dissolves, for about 5 minutes.

2. Sieve the mixture into a bowl. Add milk, lemon juice, and cinnamon. Transfer into an airtight container, freeze for 4 hours or overnight.

3. Remove from the freezer, break into chunks and add to a blender, process until smooth. Transfer back to the container and freeze for 1 hour.

4. Serve and enjoy!

Nutritional Info (per serving): 124 calories; 2.1 g fat; 24 g total carbs; 3.6 g protein

Keto Low Carb Ice Creams

Low Carb Vanilla Ice Cream

Preparation time: 3-4 hours

Cooking time: 30 minutes

Servings: 4

Ingredients

- 3 tablespoons powdered Swerve sweetener
- 1/8 teaspoon salt
- 1/2 teaspoon vanilla extract
- 1.5 cups heavy cream
- 1.5 tablespoons vodka

For sugar-free condensed milk:

- 1.5 cups heavy whipping cream
- 1/4 cup powdered Swerve Sweetener
- 2 tablespoons butter
- 1/2 teaspoon xanthan gum

Instructions

1. Bring whipping cream to a boil in a pan. Simmer over low heat for 30 minutes.

2. Turn the heat off and add butter and sweetener to the cream, stir well to combine. Add xanthan gum and whisk well to combine. Let cool.

3. Whisk in 3 tablespoons powdered Swerve sweetener, 1.5 cups heavy cream, 1/8 teaspoon salt, 1/2 teaspoon vanilla extract, and 1.5 tablespoons vodka into the condensed milk mixture.

4. Transfer the mixture to a container and freeze for 1 hour. After 1 hour, remove it from the freezer and mash everything well with a fork and freeze for 1 more hour. Freeze for at least 4 hours until firm.

5. Serve and enjoy!

Nutritional Info (per serving): 319 calories; 31.4 g fat; 2.4 g total carbs; 1.7 g protein

Low Carb Mocha Ice Cream

Preparation time: 3-4 hours

Cooking time: 15 minutes

Servings: 4

Ingredients

- 15 drops of liquid Stevia
- 1/4 teaspoon xanthan gum

- 1 cup of coconut milk
- 1 tablespoon instant coffee
- 1/4 cup heavy cream
- 2 tablespoons cocoa powder
- 2 tablespoons erythritol

Instructions

1. Add all ingredients except for xanthan gum to a container and mix well with an immersion blender.
2. Add in xanthan gum slowly and mix well until the mixture is slightly thicker.
3. Transfer ice cream mixture to a container and freeze for 40 minutes. After 40 minutes, remove it from the freezer and stir very well with a fork or a spatula.

4. Freeze for another 40 minutes. Repeat the process 3-4 more times or until the ice cream is frozen.

5. Garnish with mint and serve!

Nutritional Info (per serving): 175 calories; 14.9 g fat; 6.6 g total carbs; 2.5 g protein

Brown Butter Pecan Ice Cream

Preparation time: 3-4 hours

Cooking time: 10 minutes

Servings: 4

Ingredients

- 5 tablespoons butter
- 1/4 teaspoon xanthan gum

- 1.5 cups unsweetened coconut milk
- 25 drops of liquid Stevia
- 1/4 cup heavy whipping cream
- 1/4 cup pecans, crushed

Instructions

1. Melt butter in a pan over low heat. Add in 1/4 cup heavy whipping cream, 1/4 cup crushed pecans, and 25 drops of liquid Stevia. Stir well.
2. Then add this butter mixture to a big bowl along with 1.5 cups unsweetened coconut milk and 1/4 teaspoon xanthan gum.
3. Transfer the ice cream mixture to a container and freeze for 40 minutes. After 40 minutes, remove it from the freezer and stir very well with a fork or a spatula.
4. Freeze for another 40 minutes. Repeat the process 3-4 more times or until the ice cream is frozen.

5. Serve and enjoy!

Nutritional Info (per serving): 355 calories; 36 g fat; 4.4 g total carbs; 2 g protein

Butterscotch Sea Salt Ice Cream

Preparation time: 3-4 hours

Cooking time: 10 minutes

Servings: 4

Ingredients

- 1 teaspoon flaked sea salt
- 1 cup of coconut milk

- 1/2 teaspoon xanthan gum
- 1/4 cup sour cream
- 2 tablespoons erythritol
- 1/4 cup heavy whipping cream
- 25 drops liquid Stevia
- 3 tablespoons butter
- 2 teaspoons butterscotch flavoring
- 2 tablespoons vodka
- 1/4 cup walnuts, crushed

Instructions

1. Add all the ingredients to a bowl except the butter and mix well with an immersion blender.
2. Add butter to a pan placed over medium-low heat, cook until slightly browned. Transfer it to the bowl

with the ice cream mixture and blend again with an immersion blender.

3. Transfer the ice cream mixture to a container and freeze for 40 minutes. After 40 minutes, remove it from the freezer and stir very well with a fork or a spatula.

4. Freeze for another 40 minutes. Repeat the process 3-4 more times or until the ice cream is frozen.

5. Top with chopped walnuts and serve!

Nutritional Info (per serving): 274 calories; 24.7 g fat; 5 g total carbs; 1.4 g protein

Low Carb Chocolate Ice Cream

Preparation time: 4 6 hours

Cooking time: 5 minutes

Servings: 4

Ingredients

- 1/4 teaspoon cream of tartar

- 1.25 cups heavy whipping cream, or coconut cream

- 5.3 oz. 85% or 90% dark chocolate, broken into pieces

- 1 tablespoon sugar-free vanilla extract

- 1.8 oz. cocoa butter

- 1/2 cup powdered Erythritol or Swerve

- 4 eggs (whites and yolks separated)

Instructions

1. Add cocoa butter to a pan along with chocolate and melt completely. Once done, let it cool to room temperature.

2. Meanwhile, beat together egg whites and 1/4 teaspoon cream of tartar in a bowl. Once thickened, add in 1/2 cup powdered Erythritol slowly. Beat well until stiff peaks form.

3. Take another bowl and whisk the cream until stiff peaks form.

4. Combine 1 tablespoon sugar-free vanilla extract and the egg yolks in a separate bowl.

5. Add about a third of the fluffy egg whites to the melted, cooled chocolate and mix well. Then fold in the remaining egg whites. Stir in the egg yolk-vanilla mixture slowly.

6. Fold in 1.25 cups heavy whipping cream with a spatula.

7. Transfer to a parchment-lined baking dish and freeze until set for 4 to 6 hours.

8. Serve and enjoy!

Nutritional Info (per serving): 267 calories; 25 g fat; 5.5 g total carbs; 5 g protein

Vegan Ice Creams

Watermelon Mint Ice Cream

Preparation time: 5 hours

Cooking time: 0 minutes

Servings: 4

Ingredients

- 1 cup coconut cream

- 2 tablespoons maple syrup

- 5 cups watermelon chunks, frozen

- A handful of fresh mint

- Pinch of salt

Instructions

1. Add all the ingredients to a food processor or a blender and blend until smooth and creamy.

2. Transfer the ice cream mixture to a large container and freeze for 4 hours or overnight.

3. Take it out of the freezer, break it into chunks and add it to a blender, process until smooth. Transfer it back to the container and freeze it for 1 hour.

4. Serve and enjoy!

Nutritional Info (per serving): 297 calories; 11 g fat; 13 g total carbs; 2 g protein

Vegan Mango Ice Cream

Preparation time: 5-6 hours

Cooking time: 0 minutes

Servings: 4

Ingredients

- 24 oz. mango chunks, frozen
- 10 oz. raspberries, frozen

- 1-2 containers (5.3 oz.) vanilla dairy-free yogurt

Instructions

1. Thaw mango and raspberries for a few minutes and transfer to a food processor along with yogurt. Blend well until smooth, then transfer to a loaf pan or a container.

2. Transfer the ice cream mixture to a large container and freeze for 4 hours or overnight.

3. Take it out of the freezer, break it into chunks and add it to a blender, process until smooth. Transfer it back to the container and freeze it for 1 hour.

4. Serve and enjoy!

Nutritional Info (per serving): 128 calories; 2 g fat; 26 g total carbs; 4 g protein

Vegan Chocolate Ice Cream

Preparation time: 3-4 hours

Cooking time: 10 minutes

Servings: 4

Ingredients

- 1/2 cup cacao powder
- 1/4–1/2 teaspoon sea salt

- 1 can (15 oz.) full-fat coconut milk
- 1 teaspoon vanilla extract
- 2 cups almond milk
- 1 to 4 tablespoons maple syrup
- 1/3 cup tapioca starch

Instructions

1. Blend all the ingredients in a food processor until combined and transfer it to a saucepan. Bring the mixture to a boil, stirring constantly. Once it starts bubbling, whisk for a few minutes more until thickened.
2. Turn the heat off and transfer the mixture to a container/bowl. Refrigerate for at least 4 hours or until chilled completely.
3. Remove it from the freezer and stir very well with a fork or a spatula.

4. Freeze for another 40 minutes. Repeat the process 3-4 more times or until the ice cream is frozen.

5. Serve and enjoy!

Nutritional Info (per serving): 279 calories; 18 g fat; 28 g total carbs; 5 g protein

Fudgy Marble Fudge Gelato

Preparation time: 4-5 hours

Cooking Time: 0 minutes

Servings: 4

Ingredients:

- 1 can (15 oz.) regular coconut milk + 1/2 cup
- 1 can (15 oz.) light coconut milk

- 2/3 cup coconut nectar

- 1 tablespoon vanilla extract

- 1/4 teaspoon salt

- 1 cup vegan dark chocolate chips, melted

Instructions

1. Add all the ingredients except for the chocolate to a blender and process until smooth. Add the chocolate chips mixture, stir slightly.

2. Transfer the ice cream mixture to a shallow but large enough container and freeze for 40 minutes. After 40 minutes, take the ice cream out from the freezer and break the ice crust on the surface. Mash everything well with a fork.

3. Freeze for another 40 minutes. Repeat the process one more time and freeze for the last 30-40 minutes. Remove the gelato from the freezer at least 5-10 minutes before serving.

4. Serve and enjoy!

Nutritional Info (per serving): 534 calories; 53.7 g fat; 14 g total carbs; 5 g protein

Chocolate Chunk Beet Ice Cream

Preparation time: 5-6 hours

Cooking time: 0 minutes

Servings: 4

Ingredients

- 1/4 cup agave
- 3 tablespoons vegan dark chocolate, chopped

- 18 oz. beets, cooked, chopped
- 1 piece of ginger, peeled
- 1 cup full-fat coconut milk

Instructions

1. Add 1/4 cup agave to a food processor along with the ginger, coconut milk, and cooked beets. Blend well until smooth.
2. Transfer the ice cream mixture to a container and freeze for 40 minutes. After 40 minutes, remove it from the freezer and stir very well with a fork or a spatula.
3. Freeze for another 40 minutes. Repeat the process 3-4 more times or until the ice cream is frozen.
4. Stir in 3 tablespoons chopped dark chocolate chunks and freeze for at least two hours more. Once done, let it melt for 5 to 10 minutes and serve.

Nutritional Info (per serving): 319 calories; 31.4 g fat; 2.4 g total carbs; 1.7 g protein

For Adults

Rum Cherry Ice Cream

Preparation time: 3-4 hours

Cooking time: 40 minutes

Servings: 4

Ingredients

- 1 lb. fresh cherries, pitted and halved
- 2 cups heavy cream
- 1.5 teaspoons pure vanilla extract
- 6 egg yolks
- 1/3 cup plus 2 tablespoons granulated sugar, divided
- 1/4 teaspoon kosher salt
- 2 to 3 tablespoons dark rum
- 1/2 cup light corn syrup
- 1 cup whole milk

Instructions

1. Add 1/3 cup of sugar to a saucepan along with the cherries and simmer over low heat until the cherries have softened, for about 8 to 10 minutes, stirring occasionally.

2. Once done, strain the syrup into a separate bowl and keep it aside.

3. Transfer the cherries to another bowl and add 2 to 3 tablespoons of dark rum. Stir well.

4. Now bring both cherries and syrup to room temperature, then refrigerate them until well-chilled, covered.

5. Combine 1/2 cup light corn syrup, 1/4 teaspoon kosher salt, 1 cup whole milk, and 2 cups heavy cream in a heavy saucepan and cook at low heat stirring often, until the mixture reaches a temperature of about 175 °F. Then turn the heat off.

6. Take another bowl and whisk together the remaining sugar and egg yolks. Whisk in one-third of warm milk slowly and gradually.

7. Stir in the yolk mixture to the pot and stir well until combined. Cook at low, until it is thick. Do not boil.

8. Strain custard into a large bowl and add 1.5 teaspoons pure vanilla extract. Stir well.

9. Let it stand at room temperature for 10 to 15 minutes. Wrap with plastic and refrigerate for at least 4 hours until well-chilled.

10. Stir in the leftover cherry syrup into the custard. Transfer the ice cream mixture to a container and freeze for 40 minutes. After 40 minutes, remove it from the freezer and stir very well with a fork or a spatula.

11. Freeze for another 40 minutes. Repeat the process for 3-4 more times or until ice cream is frozen.

12. Serve topped with reserved cherries.

Nutritional Info (per serving): 415 calories; 26 g fat; 40 g total carbs; 4 g protein

Mojito Ice Cream

Preparation time: 3-4 hours

Cooking time: 20 minutes

Servings: 4

Ingredients

For the lime syrup:

- 4 tablespoons granulated sugar

- 1/3 cup freshly squeezed lime juice

For the cornstarch slurry:

- 2 tablespoons whole milk
- 1 tablespoon + 1 teaspoon cornstarch

For the ice cream base:

- 2 tablespoons light corn syrup
- 3 tablespoons coconut rum
- 2 cups whole milk
- 5 tablespoons lime syrup
- 1 cup heavy cream
- 1 heaping cup of mint leaves, chopped
- 3/4 cup granulated sugar
- 4 limes, zested

Instructions

1. Add sugar to a pan along with lime juice. Simmer for 3 to 5 minutes, until the sugar dissolves. Turn off the heat and let it cool at room temperature. Refrigerate it in a sealed container until ready to use.

2. Combine the milk and cornstarch together in a bowl and stir well until dissolved. Keep it aside too.

3. Add ice water to a large bowl. Place an open one-gallon Ziploc bag inside the bowl and keep it aside.

4. Add 2 cups whole milk, lime zest, heavy cream, corn syrup, and 3/4 cup granulated sugar to a pan. Bring everything to a boil, stirring all the time. Then turn down the heat and add in cornstarch slurry slowly. Whisk vigorously for a few minutes, until thickened. Turn off the heat and add in mint leaves.

5. Now pour this mixture into a Ziploc bag in an ice bath. Seal it and let it cool completely.

6. Once done, refrigerate this bag overnight or for at least 5 hours.

7. Strain the mixture to extract as much liquid as possible. Add in lime syrup and stir well until incorporated.

8. Stir in 3 tablespoons of coconut rum. Transfer the ice cream mixture to a container and freeze for 40 minutes. After 40 minutes, remove it from the freezer and stir very well with a fork or a spatula.

9. Freeze for another 40 minutes. Repeat the process 3-4 more times or until the ice cream is frozen.

10. Serve and enjoy!

Nutritional Info (per serving): 447 calories; 15 g fat; 79 g total carbs; 5 g protein

Moscato Ice Cream

Preparation time: 3-4 hours

Cooking time: 0 minutes

Servings: 4

Ingredients

- 1 box (3.4 oz.) instant vanilla pudding mix
- 3/4 cup fresh blueberries

- 1 cup Barefoot Moscato

- 3/4 cup fresh raspberries, chopped

- 1 cup granulated sugar

- 1 pint cold heavy whipping cream

Instructions

1. Place a bowl from a stand mixer into a freezer and freeze until cold.

2. Add instant vanilla pudding mix to another bowl along with 1 cup Moscato and 1 cup granulated sugar. Whisk well and keep it aside.

3. Now take out the bowl from the freezer. Whip chilled whipping cream for 80 to 90 seconds until stiff peaks form.

4. Reduce the speed and pour in the pudding mixture slowly and process until combined.

5. Stir in the fresh berries with a spatula. Transfer the ice cream to a tupperware container or large loaf pan. Cover with plastic wrap tightly.

6. Freeze for 12 hours at least or overnight.

7. Serve the Moscato ice cream with fresh berries. Enjoy!

Nutritional Info (per serving): 256 calories; 15 g fat; 29 g total carbs; 1 g protein

Stout Ice Cream with Bittersweet Hot Fudge

Preparation time: 4-6 hours

Cooking time: 25 minutes

Servings: 4

Ingredients

- 1/2 cup of sugar

- 12 oz. stout beer
- 2 cups heavy cream
- 1/2 teaspoon sea salt
- 6 egg yolks
- 1 teaspoon vanilla extract

For Bittersweet Hot Fudge:

- 3 oz. bittersweet chocolate (70% cacao), chopped
- 3 tablespoons light corn syrup
- 1/4 cup heavy whipping cream

Instructions

1. Add cream to a saucepan and heat over medium-high heat. Stir in half a teaspoon of salt and 1/4 cup of sugar.
2. In the meantime, whisk together ¼ cup of sugar and egg yolks in a separate bowl. Once cream begins to steam, turn the heat down.

3. Add ¼ cup of hot cream to a bowl with egg yolks and whisk well. Then add in another ¾ cup of cream (1/4 cup at a time).

4. Once eggs have tempered, add the cream and egg mixture back into the warm cream and stir well. Heat for about 5 minutes at low heat, stirring constantly. The mixture should become thick.

5. Turn the heat off and stir in 1 teaspoon vanilla extract and 12 oz. stout beer. Transfer the mixture to a fridge and chill for 1-2 hours.

6. Transfer the ice cream mixture to a container and freeze for 40 minutes. After 40 minutes, remove it from the freezer and stir very well with a fork or a spatula.

7. Freeze for another 40 minutes. Repeat the process 3-4 more times or until the ice cream is frozen.

8. **To make bittersweet hot fudge**: Add chocolate to a preheated boiler and stir until melted. Turn the heat down and stir in 1/4 cup

heavy cream and 3 tablespoons light corn syrup. Serve ice cream with hot fudge.

Nutritional Info (per serving): 636 calories; 46 g fat; 47 g total carbs; 11 g protein

Piña Colada Sorbet

Preparation time: 5 hours

Cooking time: 0 minutes

Servings: 4

Ingredients

- 2/3 cup granulated sugar
- 1/2 teaspoon coconut extract

- 1 fresh pineapple, cubed

- 2 tablespoons dark rum

- 1 cup light canned coconut milk

- 1 lime, juiced

Instructions

1. Add all the ingredients to a blender and process well until smooth. Refrigerate until cold.

2. Transfer the ice cream mixture to a large container and freeze for 4 hours or overnight.

3. Take it out of the freezer, break it into chunks and add it to a blender, process until smooth. Transfer it back to the container and freeze for 1 hour.

4. Serve and enjoy!

Nutritional Info (per serving): 203 calories; 2 g fat; 43 g total carbs; 2 g protein

Coffee Rum Ice Cream

Preparation time: 3-4 hours

Cooking time: 0 minutes

Servings: 4

Ingredients

- 4 oz. dark rum

- 8 scoops vanilla ice cream (you can use the recipe from this book - Vanilla Ice Cream recipe, page 13)
- 4 cups brewed coffee, at room temperature
- 1/4 cup semisweet chocolate chips, melted
- 1/2 cup coffee-flavored liqueur

Instructions

1. Combine 1/2 cup coffee-flavored liqueur to a measuring cup along with 4 cups brewed coffee and dark rum.
2. Mix the vanilla ice cream with the rum coffee mixture, transfer the ice cream mixture to a container and freeze for 40 minutes. After 40 minutes, remove it from the freezer and stir very well with a fork or a spatula.
3. Freeze for another 40 minutes. Top with melted chocolate and enjoy!

Nutritional Info (per serving): 148 calories; 22 g fat; 3 g total carbs; 2 g protein

Prosecco Ice Cream

Preparation time: 4-5 hours

Cooking time: 0 minutes

Servings: 4

Ingredients

- 2 tablespoons honey
- 2 tablespoons Prosecco

- 2 cups heavy cream

- 1 can (14.5 oz.) sweetened condensed milk

Instructions

1. Beat heavy cream in a stand mixer for about 5 minutes, until stiff peaks form.

2. Fold in 2 tablespoons of honey and sweetened condensed milk, process until combined well. Then add in 2 tablespoons Prosecco.

3. Transfer this mixture to a loaf pan. Freeze for 4 to 5 hours.

4. Just before serving, let it soften for 10 minutes, then serve and enjoy.

Nutritional Info (per serving): 306 calories; 25.8 g fat; 16 g total carbs; 5 g protein

Margarita Pops

Preparation time: 5-6 hours

Cooking time: 0 minutes

Servings: 4

Ingredients

- 1 tablespoon orange liqueur
- 1/2 cup fresh lime juice

- 1/2 can (14 oz.) sweetened condensed milk

- 2 limes, sliced

- 1/2 cup of water

- 1 cup fresh or frozen strawberries

- 1/8 cup tequila

- 1 cup of frozen mango

Instructions

1. Add fresh lime juice, tequila, sweetened condensed milk, orange liqueur, and water to a large bowl. Stir well.

2. Take 2 Dixie cups and divide 1/3 of the mixture among them.

3. Transfer 1/3 of the mixture to a blender along with the mango. Add more water, if needed, and blend until creamy and smooth. Once done, divide among 2 other Dixie cups.

4. Rinse the blender and transfer the leftover base to a blender. Add in fresh or frozen strawberries and more water, if needed. Blend until smooth and equally divide among the remaining Dixie cups.

5. Take lime slices and insert popsicle sticks into each slice. Top each cup with lemon slices. There should be no room between the lime slice and the ice cream mixture. Freeze overnight or for at least 5 hours.

6. Just before serving, open the Dixie cups with scissors and remove them from the pops.

7. Serve and enjoy!

Nutritional Info (per serving): 128 calories; 3.8 g fat; 22 g total carbs; 4 g protein

Mudslide Ice Cream

Preparation time: 3-4 hours

Cooking time: 5 hours 15 minutes

Servings: 4

Ingredients

- 1 cup chocolate, chopped
- 2 tablespoons Baileys Irish Cream

- 2 cups heavy cream
- 2 tablespoons Kahlua
- 1 can (14.5-oz.) sweetened condensed milk
- 1/4 cup hot fudge sauce, plus more for serving (you can use the recipe from this book - Stout Ice Cream with Bittersweet Hot Fudge recipe, page 169)

Instructions

1. Beat heavy cream in a stand mixer for about 5 minutes, until stiff peaks form.
2. Fold in the sweetened condensed milk and stir well until combined. Then fold in 2 tablespoons Kahlua, 1 cup chopped chocolate, 1/4 cup hot fudge sauce, and 2 tablespoons Baileys Irish Cream.
3. Transfer this mixture to a loaf pan and top with more chocolate. Freeze for about 4 to 5 hours.

4. Just before serving, let it soften for 10 minutes. Serve and enjoy!

Nutritional Info (per serving): 525 calories; 29.4 g fat; 58 g total carbs; 7 g protein

Coffee Vodka Ice Cream

Preparation Time: 3-4 hours

Cooking Time: 10 minutes

Servings: 4

Ingredients

- 2 tablespoons instant coffee
- 1/2 cup vodka

- 1.5 cups water, hot
- 3 cups coconut cream
- 1.5 cups sugar
- 2 cups whipped cream, beaten until stiff peaks form
- 1 tablespoon vanilla extract

Instructions

1. Add hot water to the coffee and mix to combine. Preheat a pan over medium heat.
2. Add coconut cream, coffee, and sugar. You can also add a pinch of salt.
3. Cook for about 5 minutes, stirring constantly.
4. Remove from heat and add vodka, cream, and vanilla, stir well to combine.

5. Transfer the ice cream mixture to a container and freeze for 40 minutes. After 40 minutes, remove it from the freezer and stir very well with a fork or a spatula.

6. Freeze for another 40 minutes. Repeat the process 3-4 more times or until the ice cream is frozen.

7. Serve and enjoy!

Nutritional information (per serving): 365 calories; 16.6 g fat; 48 g total carbs; 7 g protein

Conversion Tables

VOLUME EQUIVALENTS (LIQUID)

US STANDARD	US STANDARD (OUNCES)	METRIC (APPROXIMATE)
2 tablespoons	1 fl. oz.	30 mL
¼ cup	2 fl. oz.	60 mL
½ cup	4 fl. oz.	120 mL
1 cup	8 fl. oz.	240 mL
1½ cups	12 fl. oz.	355 mL
2 cups or 1 pint	16 fl. oz.	475 mL
4 cups or 1 quart	32 fl. oz.	1 L
1 gallon	128 fl. oz.	4 L

VOLUME EQUIVALENTS (DRY)

US STANDARD	METRIC (APPROXIMATE)
⅛ teaspoon	0.5 mL
¼ teaspoon	1 mL
½ teaspoon	2 mL
¾ teaspoon	4 mL
1 teaspoon	5 mL
1 tablespoon	15 mL
¼ cup	59 mL
⅓ cup	79 mL
½ cup	118 mL
⅔ cup	156 mL
¾ cup	177 mL
1 cup	235 mL
2 cups or 1 pint	475 mL
3 cups	700 mL
4 cups or 1 quart	1 L

TEMPERATURES

FAHRENHEIT (F)	CELSIUS (C) (APPROXIMATE)
250°F	120°C
300°F	150°C
325°F	165°C
350°F	180°C
375°F	190°C
400°F	200°C
425°F	220°C
450°F	230°C

WEIGHT

US STANDARD	METRIC (APPROXIMATE)
½ ounce	15 g
1 ounce	30 g
2 ounces	60 g
4 ounces	115 g
8 ounces	225 g
12 ounces	340 g
16 ounces or 1 pound	455 g

Other books by Helen Pearson: